SPIRITUAL WARFARE IS REAL

STUDY GUIDE

SPIRITUAL WARFARE IS REAL

STUDY GUIDE | FIVE SESSIONS

JIM CYMBALA

with Kevin and Sherry Harney

HarperChristian Resources

Spiritual Warfare Is Real Study Guide
© 2021 by Jim Cymbala

Requests for information should be addressed to:
HarperChristian Resources, 3900 Sparks Dr. SE, Grand Rapids, Michigan 49546

ISBN 978-0-310-13511-1 (softcover)
ISBN 978-0-310-13512-8 (ebook)

HarperChristian Resources titles may be purchased in bulk for church, business, fundraising, or ministry use. For information, please e-mail ResourceSpecialist@ChurchSource.com.

First Printing May 2021 / Printed in the United States of America

CONTENTS

INTRODUCTION

A CALL TO WAKE UP

C. S. Lewis wrote his classis work, *The Screwtape Letters*, in an effort to help modern-minded Christians recognize the reality of spiritual warfare and the tactics of the enemy of our soul. These letters first appeared in a weekly religious newspaper in 1941 and then in book form in 1942. They were a wake-up call to believers who had grown numb to the reality of their spiritual enemy.

Each letter is written as if it was penned by a senior demon (Uncle Screwtape) to his demonic protégé (Wormwood). Each one reveals a specific aspect of the spiritual battle between the forces of hell and ordinary people who walk in this world. Why would such a great Christian thinker as Lewis feel the need to write these letters and publish them for the consumption of every-day Christians?

The answer is simple. We are prone to doze off, fall asleep, and forget that we are in the middle of a war! Satan loves it this way! So, people like C. S. Lewis write to wake us up and get our attention. There is a real spiritual world, an actual enemy of our soul, and we need to wake up and get in the fight. If we fail to do this, we do so at our own peril.

In 1977, a generation after Lewis wrote *The Screwtape Letters*, a passionate young Christian artist named Keith Green wrote a song with the same goal in mind. He wanted to wake up the groggy Christians in his generation who did not recognize the serious spiritual battle raging all around them. Green wrote his song in the first person, through the voice of Satan. Reflect on these piercing words that come at the end of the chorus:

> *You know, it's getting very simple now*
> *'Cause no one believes in me anymore!*

Linger on that final line. *"No one believes in me anymore."* Let the words sink in. Why did C. S. Lewis write *The Screwtape Letters*? Why would Keith Green pen and sing such dark words in a song called "Satan's Boast"? Why are you reading this introduction to a five-week study on spiritual warfare?

Because the battle is real. Our enemy is still at work. We need to wake up!

Pause right now and say a prayer from the depth of your heart:

> *God of heaven, give me a bold spirit and courage to face the*
> *reality of spiritual warfare. Wake me up! Prepare me for*
> *the battle. I am yours. I am ready to stand, to fight, and to*
> *celebrate your victory.*

Let the truth of Scripture grab you by the shoulders and shake you awake.

> For our struggle is not against flesh and blood, but against
> the rulers, against the authorities, against the powers of this
> dark world and against the spiritual forces of evil in the heav-
> enly realms.
>
> (EPHESIANS 6:12)

Be alert and of sober mind. Your enemy the devil prowls around like a roaring lion looking for someone to devour. Resist him, standing firm in the faith, because you know that the family of believers throughout the world is undergoing the same kind of sufferings.

(1 PETER 5:8–9)

HOW TO USE THIS GUIDE

The *Spiritual Warfare Is Real* video study is designed to be experienced in a group setting such as a Bible study, Sunday school class, or any small-group gathering. However, if you are going through this study on your own, you can still make use of the study materials and questions after you watch the video by streaming video access on the inside front cover of this guide or by the DVD.

Each session begins with a brief opening reflection and "talk about it" questions to get you and your group thinking about the topic. You will then watch a video with pastor Jim Cymbala and jump into some directed small-group discussion, unless your group decides to watch the video ahead of time through streaming access provided on the inside front cover of this guide. You will close each session with a time of prayer as a group.

To get the most out of your group experience, keep the following points in mind. First, the real growth in this study will happen during your small-group time. This is where you will process the content of Jim Cymbala's message, ask questions, and learn from others as you hear what God is doing in their lives. For this reason, it is important for you to be fully committed to the group and attend each session so you can build trust and rapport with the other members. If you choose to only "go through the motions," or if you refrain from participating, there is a lesser chance you will find what you're looking for during this study.

Second, remember that the goal of your small group is to serve as a place where people can share, learn about God, and build intimacy and friendship. For this reason, seek to make your group a "safe place." This means being honest about your thoughts and feelings and listening carefully to everyone else's opinion. (If you are a group leader, there are additional instructions and resources in the back of the book for leading a productive discussion group.)

Third, resist the temptation to "fix" a problem someone might be having or to correct his or her theology, as that's not the purpose of your small-group time. Also, keep everything your group shares confidential. This will foster a rewarding sense of community in your group and create a place where people can heal, be challenged, and grow spiritually.

Following your group time, maximize the impact of the course with the additional between-session studies. For each session, you may wish to complete the personal study all in one sitting or spread it out over a few days (for example, working on it a half-hour a day on four different days that week). Note that if you are unable to finish (or even start!) your between-sessions personal study, you should still attend the group study video session. You are still wanted and welcome at the group even if you don't have your "homework" done.

Keep in mind that the videos, discussions, and activities are simply meant to kick-start your imagination, so you are not only open to what God wants you to hear but also how to apply it to your life. As you go through this study, be watching for what God is saying as it relates to approaching the throne of God's grace, receiving mercy, finding his peace, praying with faith, persevering in prayer for the answer, and praying together as a church.

OF NOTE

The quotations in this guide were taken from the video series and Jim Cymbala's teaching on spiritual warfare. The other resources in this guide—including the session introductions, small-group questions, and between-sessions materials—were written by Kevin and Sherry Harney in collaboration with Jim Cymbala. If you are a group leader, additional instructions and resources have been provided in the back of this guide to help you lead your group members through the study.

KNOW YOUR ENEMY

In the early 2020s, people in San Francisco started putting signs in the windows of their cars saying things like "I have nothing of value in my car, please don't break my windows." Or, "My car doors are unlocked and there is nothing to take." Why would they do this? Because a growing number of cars parked on the streets (even in populated and well-lit areas) were being robbed. Thieves were smashing windows to go through the car and take things. Many of these cars had nothing to steal, but their owners ended up paying more for car insurance and deductibles because of smashed windows. As they understood their enemy (local car burglars), they simply explained that their car had nothing to take and tried politely asking them to refrain from breaking the windows.

When we know a threat is imminent, when we understand the enemy, we can be prepared to fight back. Imagine you found out that termites or carpenter ants were ravaging the very structure of your home. You would learn about these tiny and subtle enemies and do what was necessary to fight them off.

Every Christian needs to recognize and understand the enemy of their soul. If we are going to fight back, we must be prepared to enter the battle. We are wise to study the tactics and ways of Satan and learn how to stand strong against him and his demonic

1

workers. If we bury our head in the sand, like the proverbial ostrich, we don't become safe because we can't see the incoming attack. We just become a big target. Ignoring the enemy never makes him go away. Being afraid is natural but turning to run away just exposes our back. What we need to do is stand in the supernatural name of the resurrected Jesus Christ and fight back in the power of the Holy Spirit.

Step one: know your enemy. Let's get started!

Satan is a spiritual being who tempts everyone, all the time, toward evil. He is the cause of all the evil in the world and rules over a horde of demonic beings.

TALK ABOUT IT

➤ When you think of the devil, what images, pictures, and ideas come to your mind? If you were to talk openly about the reality and presence of Satan and demons with the average person on the street, how do you think they would respond?

Unless Jesus was a total liar and fraud, Satan is just as real as God.

WATCH VIDEO SESSION ONE

(Either use the DVD or your streaming video access on the inside front cover.)

Video Teaching Notes

Use the space provided below to write down notes, ideas, observations, or questions that hit you as you listen to Jim's teaching:

The power, glory, and victory of God

Who is Satan and what is he doing?

Satan can't compare to God

God is omnipresent, the devil is not.
God is omniscient, the devil is not.
God is omnipotent, the devil is not.

The devil's approach . . . subtle and stealthy

God's kingdom vs. Satan's kingdom

The darkness of Satan's kingdom
was overcome by the light of Jesus Christ.

Satan has no feelings, no compassion, and shows no mercy

Never drop your guard

Darkness vs. light

A Story . . . God's power can overcome the greatest of evil

VIDEO DISCUSSION

After watching this week's video teaching on spiritual warfare, go deeper into this topic by talking with your group members using these questions and conversation prompters:

1. What are ways we can stand strong against the devil's efforts to tempt and harm our lives and the lives of the people we love?

2. **Read Ephesians 6:10–18.** It is clear that the devil has tactics and schemes to tempt and attack God's people (even Jesus). How does this make you feel and how does it wake you up to the need to be aware of his tactics and efforts?

3. **Read 1 Peter 5:8–9.** The devil prowls like a roaring lion and disguises himself as an angel of light. He is deceptive and stealthy. What are ways we can identify the presence and work of the enemy when he is lurking and sneaking around our world and life?

4. The devil does not care what it takes to draw you away from God and distract you from standing strong in faith. What are some of the distractions, enticements, and lures Satan uses to draw you away from the God who protects and loves us?

A Christian cannot be inhabited by the Holy Spirit and at the same time by an evil spirit.

5. Jim mentions that we drop our guard when we "are not in the Word, not walking in Christian community, and not thinking about Jesus." How have you seen spiritual attack increase in your life when you are drifting away from the patterns and behaviors that keep you closely connected to Jesus?

Satan looks for any weakness, any sign of a limp, any open door, and then he attacks without mercy.

6. What are decisions we can make each day that will move us into God's kingdom of light and actually help his kingdom come where we live, eat, work, play, and go to church.

Satan is called the god of this world because he has influence over so much that happens around us.

7. What can you do to stay closer to Jesus and his people so that you are less of a target for the attacks and enticements of Satan? How can your group members support and help fortify you as you stand against the attacks of the enemy?

CLOSING PRAYER

Take time as a group to step into the battle as you . . .

- Lift up passionate and joy-filled prayers celebrating the victory of Jesus and the ever-present power of the Holy Spirit.
- Ask God to open your mind to understand the reality and tactics of the enemy against your life, family, church, and community.
- Ask the Spirit of the Living God to grant daily power to resist the enemy and fight any and every attack he brings against you.
- Thank God for past victories he has won on your behalf and for ways he has protected and provided for you in the midst of the battles.

When the light of Jesus enters our life, his very presence dispels darkness.

BETWEEN SESSIONS

PERSONAL REFLECTION

Take time in personal reflection to think about the following
questions . . .

- How has the power and presence of Jesus delivered and
  protected me from the attacks of the enemy throughout
  my life?
- What are repeated and specific strategies that Satan uses
  against me? What can I do to prepare for these attacks
  and stand against them in the victorious power of Jesus?
- What are ways I can partner with God to help his
  kingdom come and his will be done on earth as it is in
  heaven (in my life, home, church, and community)?

Journal, Reflections, and Notes

_____

_____

_____

_____

_____

_____

_____

_____

_____

_____

_____

_____

_____

_____

_____

_____

_____

_____

_____

_____

_____

_____

_____

_____

**The darkness of Satan's kingdom has been overcome
by the light of Jesus Christ.**

PERSONAL ACTIONS

Daily Check-In and Review

Since the devil is always prowling around seeking someone to devour and never ceases his efforts to distract, discourage, and tempt us, we need to make time every day to check in with God and ensure we are not under the attack of our enemy.

Consider taking these steps at the start of each day:

1. Reflect on the previous day and ask, "Are there ways I fell into the enticements of the enemy?" If you identify any, confess them and pray for eyes to see these enticements in the future. Also ask for the power of the Holy Spirit to help you say no the next time you face this same temptation.
2. Pray through the day ahead and ask for the Spirit of God to show you any places the enemy might be getting ready to attack.
3. Ask for the power of Jesus to protect you from the work of the enemy in your life.
4. Pray for the victory of Jesus and the glory of his resurrection power to guide you through the day ahead.

Keep notes of specific areas you have faced temptation and how you were able to stand strong in the power of Jesus:

_____

_____

_____

_____

_____

_____

Fortifying Places of Weakness

Satan is like a lion looking for the zebra or antelope with any injury that slows it down and makes it easy to catch. With merciless attention he watches the mass of people moving through life and he pounces on those who are weak, injured, and vulnerable. Followers of Jesus must identify the areas in their life where there is a crack in their integrity, a recurring bad habit, a lull in their personal time with Jesus, opening their heart and mind to media that compromises their purity, anything that the enemy will use against us.

Take time to walk through a process of self-inspection so you can identify and fortify specific places of weakness in your life.

1. **Pray.** *"Lord of truth and wisdom, show me any attitude or behavior in my life that weakens me and makes me an easy target for the enemy."*

2. **Identify an area** (or areas). Write down at least one area of struggle or disobedience in your life that weakens your faith and invites the attacks of Satan.

   • _____

   • _____

3. **Read Scripture.** Do an internet Bible search on the topic of struggle in your life. For example, if your area of struggle is living in fear, do a search on Bible passages about overcoming fear. If your struggle is with pornography, do a search on Bible passages about holiness and purity of mind. If your area of weakness is dishonesty, do a search on Bible passages about honesty and telling the truth.

➤ Write down the reference for 8–10 passages and one insight
from that passage:

Passage:

Insight:

Passage:

Insight:

Passage:

Insight:

Passage:

Insight:

Passage:

Insight:

Passage:

Insight:

Passage:

Insight:

Passage:

Insight:

4. **Memorize a verse.** Pick one of the verses you listed above and commit it to memory over the next week.

5. **Make a commitment.** Prayerfully commit to one action or habit that will help fortify and protect you against the attack of Satan in this area of your life.

My Commitment: _____

6. **Seek accountability.** Share your commitment with one strong Christian you trust and ask for their prayer and for them to ask you how you are doing in this area of growth each week for the next month.

7. **Pray more.** Over the coming weeks, as you seek to grow in this area of your life, pray daily for power, growth, and the victory of Jesus over the enemy.

In the name and power of Jesus we have victory over the one who comes to steal, kill, and destroy.

OVERCOMING THE ATTACK ON YOUR FAITH

Faith has fallen on hard times. People are losing faith in all sorts of things.

There was a time when professional athletes would spend their whole career playing for one team in one city. The fans knew the whole roster of players and followed their stats and careers closely. The local team players felt like members of the family. Now athletes shift from team to team and town to town based on massive salary and bonus offers. Faith in professional athletes and sports teams is simply not what it was before.

There was a time when people had faith in their governing officials. There was an inherent sense that these people were civil servants who wanted the best for their community, state, or country. Even if we did not know what was happening behind the political veil, we could trust in these leaders and have faith that they would make decisions that would serve the greater good. In those days, politicians on both sides of the aisle could maintain friendships with each other, share a meal, and work together. Something happened! All the polls show that faith in what political figures say and even promise is on a sharp decline.

In the 1970s a man by the name of Walter Cronkite was commonly called "the most trusted man in America." When he said something, people put faith in it. They took it as truth. He served as an anchorman for CBS news for almost two decades. Try to imagine any newscaster being rated as the most trusted person in an opinion poll today. Faith in the news media is in a death spiral!

Even faith in pastors and church leaders has fallen on hard times. Prominent religious figures seem to be caught in compromising situations on an all-too-frequent basis. Add to this the countless not-so-well-known pastors and church leaders who make poor choices and compromise their integrity. These leaders don't hit the endless news cycle, but they break the hearts of Christians who have trusted them.

In this time of diminishing faith and broken trust, Satan is having a party! He knows one of the best ways to attack Christians is to go after their faith. Step one in the enemy's strategy is to dismantle our faith. In a time when faith (in people and institutions) is on the decline, Satan will try to get us to question our faith in God's power, presence, and grace. We need to be ready to fight back and strengthen our faith in the God who never changes teams, who never tells a lie, and who is never unfaithful.

Satan's number one target is your faith.

TALK ABOUT IT

> ➤ What are signs that people's faith in institutions and worldly leaders is decreasing (in sports teams and players, politics, media, religion, and other areas of life)?

We will be better off and stronger if we face the spiritual reality that we are in a battle.

WATCH VIDEO SESSION TWO

(Either use the DVD or your streaming video access on the inside front cover.)

Video Teaching Notes

Use the space provided below to write down notes, ideas, observations, or questions that hit you as you listen to Jim's teaching:

Face it, we're in a fight

Everything hangs on faith

The battle between faith and discouragement

Jesus was amazed by faith

Faith receives from God all the blessings and wonderful gifts that are offered in Christ.

Fortifying faith by reading God's Word

Fortifying faith by seeking community

Faith and the realms of what has not yet happened and what is
not yet seen

Hold the hand of God

When you have faith, you are absolutely confident
about things that have not happened yet.

VIDEO DISCUSSION

After watching this week's video teaching on spiritual warfare, go deeper into this topic by talking with your group members using these questions and conversation prompters:

1. What does it mean to live by faith, and what are tangible signs that we are actually living in faith?

2. **Read Hebrews 11:1–6.** What does it mean to say, "Without faith it is impossible to please God?" How does walking in faith actually please the God who made us?

3. If the first target for Satan to attack in spiritual warfare is our faith, what are specific ways you see the enemy seeking to tear down the faith of Christians? How can we strengthen and fortify our faith so that we are ready for the attacks of Satan?

4. How does regular study of the Word of God deepen our faith? How can we orient our thinking to God's Word instead of the messages the world sends us?

5. **Read 1 John 5:1–5.** How can faith give us confidence and hope even amid all of life's challenges, problems, and disasters?

Faith brings confidence, joy, and boldness.

6. Who is a close Christian friend or family member who encourages you to believe in God and live with a confident faith? What does this person do and say that strengthens your faith? How can you follow their example?

One important lesson in spiritual warfare is to stay near people who promote faith and beware of those who tear down your faith.

7. If we are going to stand in faith, we should not focus on last year or next year but live in the present. What will help us keep our eyes on Jesus, take his hand, and faithfully walk with him right now?

Jesus was never amazed at anything on this earth except faith!

CLOSING PRAYER

Take time as a group to step into the battle as you . . .

- Ask God to deepen your faith and expand your trust in him with each passing day.
- Pray for both desire and discipline to open the Bible and read it each day. Ask God to use his Word to grow your faith in him and his promises.
- Thank God for the specific people he has placed in your life who model consistent faithfulness to Jesus.
- Ask the Holy Spirit to give you growing confidence in what he has promised that has not yet been seen.
- Prayerfully surrender all the material things God has placed in your care to be used for his glory. Also pray that these things will never be a distraction to your life of faith.

Satan is constantly enticing us to focus on material things, Jesus said we can't serve God and money.

BETWEEN SESSIONS

PERSONAL REFLECTION

Take time in personal reflection to think about the following
questions . . .

- What are some of the spiritual battles you have faced over
  the past year and how has the enemy tried to weaken your
  faith? How has God used this battle to strengthen you?
- What are some of the faith-building Scriptures you have
  read in the past month and how might you encourage
  others with these powerful Scriptures?
- With whom should you spend more time in the coming
  weeks with the express intention of encouraging each
  other in faith? What can you do to connect more with
  this person?

Journal, Reflections, and Notes

God-first living is the only way to receive the blessing we instinctively seek.

PERSONAL ACTIONS

What Discourages and Distracts Me?

Satan loves to discourage and distract God's people and keep them from walking in faith. Each of us has issues that can quickly bring us down. The enemy is tuned into what these are, so we need to be tuned in too.

Prayerfully ask the Lord to show you the two or three things that can easily discourage you. It could be when people are unkind to you, when you put on a few pounds and feel bad about yourself, when the stock market is uncertain or heading down, when the weather gets cold and dark, and so on. Satan does not care what it is—his only goal is to discourage you!

> ➤ Write down two or three things that have the potential to bring you down. Be honest:
> - _____
> - _____
> - _____

Pray for eyes to see when the enemy tries to pile on. Be prepared to stand strong even when you face these things because the Bible tells us that in life, we will have trouble.

> ➤ Pick one of these areas of potential discouragement and write
  down two or three things you can do when Satan tries to bring
  you down in these times. How can you pray, rely on Scripture,
  lean on a friend, get in community, or adjust your thinking to
  resist the temptation to lose faith?

- • _____
- • _____
- • _____

When you are full of faith, you can face anything!

Amaze Jesus and Declare Your Faith

Jesus was amazed when people had faith and declared it publicly. He delighted in expressions of faith in this faithless world.

Think about an area of life where you are really living by faith. You are focusing on the presence of Jesus in a tough situation, but you believe with confidence that God is going to guide you through, protect you, or provide what is needed.

> ➤ Write down the area of life where you are standing confidently
  in faith:

_____

_____

_____

_____

_____

_____

_____

_____

➤ Take a moment to write a short and bold declaration of faith about this area you are standing strong.

My declaration of faith:

_____

_____

_____

_____

_____

_____

_____

_____

_____

_____

_____

Make a point of telling someone that you are living with faith and are confident that God is leading you in this specific area. Your words will strengthen you and encourage them to live by faith!

If you only live by what you see in this world, you will always be overwhelmed.

Standing on God's Word

There are many ways we can get the Word of God into our hearts and minds. Try two or three of these ideas in the next week and journal about how this experience strengthens and deepens your faith.

Read each morning: Take time to read a psalm every morning and look for expressions of faith by the psalmist or examples of a faithful heart.

Read at lunchtime: Read a chapter of Proverbs each day while you have lunch and ask God to grow your wisdom so that you will live each day with faith in God no matter what your eyes see or the world says.

Read before bed: Read Hebrews 11 every night and meditate on the great examples of faith who have followed God before you and who now cheer you on as you walk in faith.

Memorize and reflect deeply: Chose a passage that is two or three verses long and commit it to memory over the next week. Put this passage in your phone or on a card where you will see it often throughout your day. Pick a passage that speaks of God's faithfulness.

Send a verse every day: As you read the Word of God each day, identify one faith-enhancing verse and send it to a few other people and encourage them to walk and live in faith.

Listen to Scripture: Replace music, podcasts, and other things you listen to during the day with listening to Scripture. You will be amazed at how much of the Bible you can ingest and internalize in a week if you use a Bible app and listen to God's truth rather than other things.

➤ How has this specific time reflecting on God's Word strengthened my faith?

_____

_____

_____

_____

_____

_____

RESISTING THE ATTACK ON LOVE

Here today and gone tomorrow. If we look back over time it is easy to recognize that styles become very popular in our world and then they disappear. In the world of fashion, every year new color palettes are in and others are out. Pants go from flared bell bottoms to skinny jeans to tattered and torn. There is no apparent rhyme or reason. An entire closet of clothes can become obsolete in a matter of a few years. If a person is really concerned about staying in step with fashion, they have to keep shopping and adjusting their wardrobe to make sure they don't embarrass themselves by wearing something that is clearly "out of style."

Popular music can move from classical to folk to rock to grunge to rap to hip hop . . . and the beat goes on. Of course, all these forms of music endure in some way, but certain styles of music seem to be huge for a time and then fall off the popular cultural radar.

Fads come and go. Some move so fast you might not have even known about them . . . but they happened. Hacky Sacks, Polaroid cameras, Pez candy, Mood Rings, digital pets (Tomagotchi), Beanie Babies, water beds, Pogs, and so many more. The thing about a fad is that it comes and goes . . . by definition.

As the years pass, the rate of change in our culture seems to be increasing. Things come and go so quickly. What is even more troubling is that some of the things that are trending downward are beautiful and essential gifts that honor God and bless the world, values such as: civility, grace, patience, kindness, forgiveness, and most of all, love! The enemy of our souls delights when these things take a hit and decrease. One of his tactics is to get people in general, and Christians specifically, to abandon any good gift that honors God.

We don't have to look very hard to realize that the devil is in a full-court press against love. As followers of Jesus, we must recognize his strategy and join our heavenly Father in loving others the way he does. This is war! Love is not a style that can come and go or a fad that can disappear. If Satan can get followers of Jesus to stop loving each other and our world, he will have a major victory. It is time for Christians to live in ways that lift up love as the standard for all we are and all we do.

One of Satan's strategic targets in his warfare against Christians is to attack love.

TALK ABOUT IT

> What are trends, fads, or styles you have seen come and go? Why is it critical that we never let love become something that fades or disappears from our daily lives?

In love, Jesus gave his life for us.

Satan is antichrist. This means that Satan is anti-love.

WATCH VIDEO SESSION THREE

(Either use the DVD or your streaming video access on the inside front cover.)

Video Teaching Notes

Use the space provided below to write down notes, ideas, observations, or questions that hit you as you listen to Jim's teaching:

An Easter Story: Where's the love?

The essence of God is unstoppable love

Satan's goal: Destroy love

In our hearts

In the world

**Social media is a hotbed of hate,
not just for people out in this world, but for Christians.**

In the church

The connection between love and sharing the good news of Jesus

Love God and walk in the light

The rest of the Story: There's the love!

Love can increase and decrease, so pray for your love to grow!

VIDEO DISCUSSION

After watching this week's video teaching on spiritual warfare, go deeper into this topic by talking with your group members using these questions and conversation prompters:

1. How have you experienced the love of God in your life and how does this fortify you and inspire you to grow in love for others?

> Despite who we are and what we've done, God's love transcends it all. God's love cannot be stopped.

2. Why is resentment, jealousy, and fear of others so easy, but real and pure love seem to be so difficult?

3. What are ways you see Satan destroying love among people in our world? What are some of his love-crushing tactics? What message does it send to the world, when as Christians, we fight and hate each other?

All hate, prejudice, racism, violence, murder, gossip, slander, and everything that is nasty and hateful comes from Satan.

4. Tell about a person you long to see become a Christian. How can you show love to this person? If you don't feel real and authentic love for this person right now, what steps can you take to grow your love and how can your group members pray for you in this process?

5. **Read 1 John 2:9–11.** When a Christian is walking in the love and light of Jesus, how does this impact the way they relate with other believers (give specific examples)? When a Christian is decreasing in love and allowing darkness into their heart, how can this impact the way they relate with their brothers and sisters in faith (give specific examples)?

There is no other way that we can represent Christ effectively without being filled with his light and love.

6. What steps can your church take to grow in love for others? What specific church actions and ministries can reveal the love of God in your community?

7. **Read John 13:34–35.** In what specific ways has God loved us and how can we follow this example as we grow in love for others? How can we pray for our group members as we seek to grow in our love for others?

We cannot effectively share the gospel if we do not love people.

CLOSING PRAYER

Take time as a group to step into the battle as you . . .

- Thank God for loving you with eternal and amazing love . . . even before you loved him.
- Lift up a prayer of thanks to God for a person who has been a long-term example of God's love in your life.
- Take a moment in *silent prayer* to confess where you have been hard-hearted and unloving toward a person or group of people.

- Ask God for strength and power to love the people in your life who are difficult and challenging.
- Pray for your church to be a place that shines the light and love of Jesus to anyone and everyone.

God, fill me, over and over again, with your love so that I can see people the way you see them and feel for them the way you feel.

BETWEEN SESSIONS

PERSONAL REFLECTION

Take time in personal reflection to think about the following questions . . .

- Are there individuals or groups of people who I have a hard time loving? Why do I feel this way?
- What do I need to confess to God or pray about to help me love these people with the love of God?
- What actions can I take to grow in love with people who God loves but I have a hard time caring for?

Journal, Reflections, and Notes

God's love is the only antidote to Satan's hate.

PERSONAL ACTIONS

A Time to Repent

Repentance is about changed attitudes, heart condition, and actions. Take a moment to identify a person or group of people that you have a hard time loving. Be humble and honest before God as you invite the Holy Spirit to search your heart and show you where love needs to grow.

Attitudes

➤ What are attitudes you carry in your mind about this person, group of people, or kind of people? Reflect on your disposition or outlook and pray for God to give you his perspective on this person or group of people.

Emotions

➤ Why do you feel the way you do toward this person or people group? What happened in your past? What were you taught or told? What did you experience?

Offer your fear, pain, anger, or resentment to God and ask him to heal your heart. Pray that the feelings that get in the way of you loving others will be healed and transformed to love. If you can't identify the source of these feelings, seek wisdom from a trusted Christian friend, a pastor, or a Christian counselor.

Actions

➤ Seek to identify actions you engage in that are hostile, hurtful, or harsh toward this person or people group. Really examine your behavior, responses, and words. As you identify specific actions, plan new ways to respond and pray for power to express love instead of hate.

If you want to go one step deeper, ask a trusted Christian friend to pray for you and keep you accountable in this area of desired growth. Share your plan to respond in new ways and ask them to check in and see how you are doing in your efforts to change your actions.

Learning from Jesus

Jesus loved people who were seen as unlovable, untouchable, and unworthy. Throughout the four Gospels, we see Jesus loving people with a consistent and heavenly kindness. Take time to read about some of these encounters and seek to learn lessons from Jesus, our perfect example of love.

Person: Nicodemus (Some people are excluded and hated because they are wealthy and powerful.)

Passage: John 3:1–15

Lessons from Jesus: What I learn about loving others as I look at Jesus . . .

<u>**Lesson**</u>

<u>**Lesson**</u>

<u>**Lesson**</u>

Person: Woman at the Well (Some people are avoided and excluded because they have a sketchy moral past, present, or both.)

Passage: John 4:4–26

Lessons from Jesus: What I learn about loving others as I look at Jesus . . .

<u>**Lesson**</u>

<u>**Lesson**</u>

Lesson

Person: A man with leprosy (Some people are unloved or avoided because of health or appearance issues.)
Passage: Mark 1:40–45
Lessons from Jesus: What I learn about loving others as I look at Jesus . . .

Lesson

Lesson

Lesson

Person: Zacchaeus (Some people are hated because of how they have treated others.)
Passage: Luke 19:1–10
Lessons from Jesus: What I learn about loving others as I look at Jesus . . .

Lesson

Lesson

Lesson

Person: Demon-possessed man (Some people are feared and hated because they are possessed by evil.)

Passage: Mark 5:1–20

Lessons from Jesus: What I learn about loving others as I look at Jesus . . .

Lesson

Lesson

Lesson

God's love can take the worst mess and make it into something beautiful.

This Is Love

One of the best ways we can grow our love for others is to meditate on the source of our love for others.

Read 1 John 4:7–12.

7 Dear friends, let us love one another, for love comes from God. Everyone who loves has been born of God and knows God.

> ➤ *Reflect:* What do you learn about God's love . . .

_____

_____

_____

_____

_____

8 Whoever does not love does not know God, because God is love.

> ➤ *Reflect:* What do you learn about God's love . . .

_____

_____

_____

_____

_____

_____

9 This is how God showed his love among us: He sent his one and only Son into the world that we might live through him.

➤ *Reflect:* What do you learn about God's love . . .

_____

_____

_____

_____

_____

[10] This is love: not that we loved God, but that he loved us and sent his Son as an atoning sacrifice for our sins.

➤ *Reflect:* What do you learn about God's love . . .

_____

_____

_____

_____

_____

[11] Dear friends, since God so loved us, we also ought to love one another. [12] No one has ever seen God; but if we love one another, God lives in us and his love is made complete in us.

➤ *Reflect:* What do you learn about God's love . . .

_____

_____

_____

_____

_____

Spend time in reflection and prayer as you seek to live in the truth of this passage.

PRESSING THROUGH THE ATTACK ON YOUR CALLING

A young mother says, "I don't have time to do ministry or think about God's calling on my life. I am too busy raising three kids and trying to build a marriage that honors Jesus!"

An elderly man declares, "I'm too old to have a calling and do ministry in the church. My body is growing weak and I don't have much I can give or do these days. About all I can offer is prayer for people in need."

A Christian woman who serves as an executive for a banking group admits to her pastor, "I work six days a week, travel regularly for business, and struggle to make time for my marriage and family. When you talk about each Christian having a calling and ministry, I just feel guilty! I barely have time to mentor the four businesswomen in the small group I lead every Wednesday morning before work."

A passionate high school student tells his youth leader, "I don't have any gifts or skills for ministry or to serve Jesus. I just like to encourage younger Christian guys to read their Bible, pray, and not make stupid decisions!"

A seasoned saint tells her Sunday School leader that she does not need to take the spiritual gifts class coming up at church because she is sure she does not have any gifts. The Sunday School teacher asks, "Weren't you a neo-natal nurse for thirty years, and don't you serve in the nursery every week? And, don't you volunteer to visit shut-ins and some of our home-bound church members?"

What do all five of these people have in common? What is it that they don't realize? The answer might already be clear. They all have a calling from God. Each one of them is gifted and is serving Jesus and others. The young mother has a calling to raise children to love Jesus. The elderly man has the gift of intercession and can pray powerfully for others. The businesswoman is discipling and mentoring other women in the marketplace to shine the light of Jesus. The high school student has the gift of encouragement and builds up other young men as they follow Jesus. The retired nurse now serves the youngest and oldest people in her church and brings care and compassion.

Too often Christians don't realize they have a ministry that is blessed and led by the Spirit of God. Our spiritual enemy is in the business of getting Christians to deny their calling, ignore their gifting, and refuse to serve in the name of Jesus. We need to recognize when Satan is attacking our calling. We must refuse to buy his lies. Our good and gracious God has called and gifted each of us to serve him, the church, and the world. God's plan is to mobilize every follower of Jesus for world-changing ministry. We must hear God's call on our lives and get busy serving in whatever way the Holy Spirit leads.

Satan tempted Jesus to leave his calling.
That was a strategic target of the enemy against the Savior.
It is still his evil desire for you and me.

TALK ABOUT IT

➤ Most of us will never serve on a church staff or become a pastor, but we all have a calling from God and ministry he has gifted us to do. What is your calling and how are you living it out for the glory of Jesus?

WATCH VIDEO SESSION FOUR

(Either use the DVD or your streaming video access on the inside front cover.)

Video Teaching Notes

Use the space provided below to write down notes, ideas, observations, or questions that hit you as you listen to Jim's teaching:

Satan attacked Jesus' calling, you had better believe he will attack yours

---

Satan's target is your calling. He is always trying to steal and stall the very purpose God has for your life.

The purpose of our life (a general calling)

We are called to be with him

This is what it means to be a Christian

The difference between relationship and fellowship

The importance of listening to Jesus, singing, and being thankful

Each of us has a function and purpose that is unique . . . this is our calling

We all have a gift

Use your gift

The source of true joy and peace

Joy and peace don't come from the accumulation of things.
True joy and abiding peace come from doing the will of God.

VIDEO DISCUSSION

After watching this week's video teaching on spiritual warfare, go deeper into this topic by talking with your group members using these questions and conversation prompters:

1. Tell about a time you were tempted to walk away from your God-given calling. How did you respond to this demonic enticement?

2. **Read Matthew 4:1–11.** What are some of the tactics and approaches the enemy uses to discourage us from fulfilling the calling God has placed on us? How can we battle against these enticements?

3. What is your calling and place of serving Jesus and how are you seeking to follow this call and honor the Savior? What is getting in the way of you fully engaging in this call?

A Christian is someone who has repented of their sins, been born again, and who has a real and growing relationship with Jesus.

4. What are specific tactics the enemy tries to use against you to keep you from serving Jesus and investing your time and gifts to honor the Savior?

5. **Read Mark 3:13–19.** Jesus called the twelve apostles to be with him. What is the difference between having a relationship and having fellowship? How can we be sure we are walking in fellowship with Jesus?

Jesus called his followers so that they might be with him. Then, he sent them out to preach and have authority over evil spirits. Calling number one, be with Jesus. Calling number two, serve Jesus.

6. **Read 1 Corinthians 12:12–26.** Why is each part of our body needed and important, and how is the church like a physical body? How are you using your gifting for the glory of Jesus and how can you grow in this calling?

7. Jesus was clear that he received nourishment and strength by fulfilling the call of the Father on his life. How do you get fired up, strengthened, and fortified by serving Jesus with the gifts he has given you and fulfilling his calling on your life? How can your group members pray for you as you seek to fulfill God's calling on your life?

Christ did not die on the cross so we could go to church on Sunday. He died and rose to save us and send us on his mission to change the world.

CLOSING PRAYER

Take time as a group to step into the battle as you . . .

- Pray for your group members to receive a fresh passion and commitment to discover and engage in the calling God has for them.
- Thank God for the unique call he has given you and ask for boldness and devotion to live out his call every single day of your life.
- Pray for each member of your group to recognize the tactics the enemy uses to distract them from fulfilling God's call on their lives.
- Ask God to bear great fruit through your life as you fulfill his calling and use the gifts he has given for his glory.
- Pray for yourself and your group members to have bold courage to follow God's call even when it is costly and demands more than you think you can give.

BETWEEN SESSIONS

PERSONAL REFLECTION

Take time in personal reflection to think about the following questions . . .

- What are some of the passions, abilities, and unique gifts God has given you? Remember, it is not prideful to recognize and rejoice in your God-given abilities that can be used for the glory of Jesus.
- What are ways God has used your calling and the ministry he has done through you to bless others, strengthen the church, and bring himself glory?
- Write a short prayer of thanks and praise to God for how he has worked in and through your calling.

_____

_____

_____

_____

_____

_____

_____

_____

Christ is the head. We get our directions from him.
Our part is to carry out the ministry he gives us.

Journal, Reflections, and Notes

_____

_____

_____

_____

_____

_____

_____

_____

_____

_____

_____

_____

_____

_____

_____

_____

_____

_____

_____

_____

_____

_____

PERSONAL ACTIONS

Daily Time with Jesus

Our first call is to be with Jesus, to love him, and to grow in fellowship with the Savior who has made us his own. As you seek to grow your relationship with Jesus, begin by taking note of ways you are already connecting with God through the flow of your normal day. Be honest with yourself and with God in this process . . . because you both already know the true answer to each of these questions.

Reflecting on My Connection with God

➤ *Digging into God's Word:* When, where, and how do I engage in God's Word (the Bible) in the flow of my day?

- _____
- _____
- _____
- _____
- _____
- _____

➤ *Talking with God in prayer:* What are some of the ways that I engage with God in prayer when I am alone or with others in a normal day?

- _____
- _____
- _____
- _____
- _____
- _____

➤ **Celebrating God in worship:** How do I worship God, celebrate his goodness, thank him for his provision and presence, and sing praise to him in the routine of my everyday life?

- _____
- _____
- _____
- _____
- _____

Going Deeper in My Intimacy with God

Set some specific goals and develop some practices that will deepen your friendship with Jesus and intimacy with the God who loves you. Be specific about the when and where of these new ways you will connect with God.

➤ **Digging into God's Word:** When, where, and how will I engage in God's Word (the Bible) in fresh new ways?

- _____
- _____
- _____
- _____
- _____

➤ **Talking with God in prayer:** What are some of the ways I will begin to engage with God in prayer when I am alone or with others?

- _____
- _____
- _____
- _____
- _____

> ➤ *Celebrating God in worship:* How can I begin to worship God, celebrate his goodness, thank him for his provision and presence, and sing praise to him in the routine of my everyday life?

- _____
- _____
- _____
- _____
- _____

Share your goals and commitments to grow your intimacy with God with a close and trusted Christian friend or family member. Ask them to pray for you and invite them to check in with you to see how you are growing over the coming weeks.

Our first calling is always to be with Jesus.
If we miss this calling, there is no second calling.

Explore Something New

> ➤ As you have reflected on your calling and the gifts God's Spirit has instilled in you, write down three potential ways you can serve and fulfill your calling that you have never tried before:

1. A gifting or ability God has given:

2. A gifting or ability God has given:

3. A gifting or ability God has given:

Prayerfully choose one of these potential ways you can serve and honor Jesus and give it a try sometime in the next thirty days. Explore this new way God could use you for his glory and see if it bears fruit and brings joy as you see God work in and through you.

➤ Write down what you learned about your gifting and calling through this experience:

_____
_____
_____
_____
_____
_____
_____

Study Your Church

Every church has opportunities and ministries where they need gifted Christians to serve faithfully. Our calling does not have to be lived out in the local church, but for many of God's people, the church is a great place to discover, develop, and engage their God-given call. So, consider doing some of the things suggested below as you study your church and discern if there are ways you can exercise your calling right where you gather to worship.

Check your church website: A ten-to-twenty-minute journey through your church website could expose you to ministries you don't know about, highlight areas of need, and tune you into places your gifts and abilities could be used to fulfill your calling. Prayerfully look through the church website.

Notes from my website tour:

_____

_____

_____

_____

_____

_____

_____

_____

_____

Do a prayerful walk-around: Take fifteen minutes on a Sunday or some other time the church is gathered. Walk around your church building and pray, observe, ask questions, and open your heart to prompting of the Holy Spirit. This is a wonderful way to discover needs and ministry opportunities you might have never noticed before.

Notes from my walk-around:

_____

_____

_____

_____

_____

_____

_____

_____

Talk with a ministry leader: Schedule a thirty-minute meeting with a church leader (staff or volunteer). Simply ask them what needs the church has and possible places you might serve. Don't start committing to everything, but do pray for the opportunities you learn about.

Notes from my chat with a ministry leader:

_____

_____

_____

_____

_____

_____

_____

Pray for your church leaders: Use your church's website or a church directory to get a list of leaders in your church. Then, pray for each one by name. As you learn the specifics of their particular ministry, be open for God to grow a passion in your heart or expand your interest to get more involved.

Impressions God placed on my heart as I prayed for our church leaders:

_____

_____

_____

_____

_____

_____

_____

Pay attention to announcements and church communication:
Commit to really paying attention any time church announcements are shared. Also, read any hard copy or email communications from your church. These often highlight places of need in the church.

Things I have picked up while paying closer attention to what's happening in my church:

_____

_____

_____

_____

_____

_____

_____

Let's pursue God's calling and do what he had made us to do. Then, at the end of our life, we can say, "I have fought the good fight!"

FIGHTING THROUGH THE ATTACK ON PRAYER

A power outage is no fun. All of a sudden, everything does dark. Lights go out. Refrigerators stop cooling the perishables. If it is hot, air conditioners stop working and things heat up really fast. Appliances go silent. If a home, a block, or a city experiences a power outage, everyone wants to know, *When will this end? When will the power be back on?*

If you have ever broken a leg or an arm, you know the inconvenience of spending week after week in a cast. You can't bend it, you can't use it, and as the weeks go by, your muscles wither and weaken. When the doctor finally takes off the cast, the limb that has been healing feels powerless. You have to rebuild muscles because the strength you developed through regular use is gone.

A person who experiences a serious stroke knows the intense feeling of powerlessness. In most cases, half of their body stops responding to mental cues and orders. It simply does not work! They often can't walk or take care of themselves, and in some cases they can't speak. A healthy, strong, independent person can have their whole life changed in an instant and feel the torturous pain of lacking the power to live as they have for much of their life.

When power is taken away, it is a serious moment.

The God of the universe has all power and he wants to offer every one of his children the power to live for him. Power to love others. Power to walk in holiness. Power to serve in the name of Jesus. Power to worship with passion. Power to resist temptation. And power for so much more.

Satan, the enemy of our soul, wants to cripple us, steal God's power from us, and attack the divine power supply we all need. The devil wants us weak, incapacitated, and disconnected from the staggering power of heaven. He will do whatever he can to keep us from walking and living in the divine power of the Holy Spirit. He knows that when we are plugged into the power of heaven, everything on earth changes and his power is shut down!

God grants grace, strength, and power
when people stop and ask him for it.

TALK ABOUT IT

> If you have experienced a power outage, broken limb, a stroke (or watched someone deal with the aftermath of a stroke), or faced some other loss of power, describe what it felt like.

WATCH VIDEO SESSION FIVE

(Either use the DVD or your streaming video access on the inside front cover.)

Video Teaching Notes

Use the space provided below to write down notes, ideas, observations, or questions that hit you as you listen to Jim's teaching:

Like it or not, victory only comes when there is power

Power does not just fall into our lap, we work for it

Our greatest source of power, the Holy Spirit

The Holy Spirit grants supernatural power to believe and endure when otherwise you would fall by the wayside.

Lesson #1 – We can't stand strong in our own power . . . we need the Holy Spirit!

Lesson #2 – We can do all things when the power of the Spirit is in us

We need fresh power today.
You can't live off of what God did last week.

Lesson #3 – We need regular and fresh filling of the Holy Spirit

Lesson #4 – The way we receive the power of the Spirit is through prayer

Lesson #5 – We can plug into the power outlet of prayer

Lesson #6 – We can pray in the Spirit

Satan seeks to attack us by keeping us from the power source, which is prayer.

Lesson #7 – We experience victory through prayer

Lesson #8 – We must persevere in prayer and pray in community

VIDEO DISCUSSION

After watching this week's video teaching on spiritual warfare, go deeper into this topic by talking with your group members using these questions and conversation prompters:

1. Tell about a time you saw a display of power (of any kind) that amazed you and caused awe and wonder.

2. **Read Ephesians 6:10–13.** What does it mean to be strong in the Lord and in his mighty power? Describe a time you felt the power of God alive and at work in you. What did it feel like, and what resulted from this filling of power?

Prayer is the avenue for receiving Holy Spirit power.

3. Why is it essential that we recognize the power of the Holy Spirit and that we draw on his power when we face spiritual battles?

Satan can only be overcome by greater power.
Spiritual power comes only from the Holy Spirit to fight battles.

4. In what area of your life do you need a fresh filling of the power of the Holy Spirit so that you can follow his will for your life and walk in boldness?

5. What are ways that Satan seeks to keep Christians from praying? How can we fight back against these evil tactics?

Satan knows that he is defeated
when we talk to God and tell him our needs.

6. **Read Ephesians 6:18–20.** What does the apostle Paul teach
   us about the centrality and importance of prayer in this passage? What is a next step you can take to follow this powerful
   exhortation and make prayer a larger part of your daily life?

7. Consider people who support you in prayer regularly and how
   God has empowered you through their prayers. Share a story of
   a time you saw the power of God unleashed in your life through
   the prayers of faithful people who came next to you and held
   up your arms (supported you in prayer).

Prayer links us up with God, and with God, everything is possible.

CLOSING PRAYER

Take time as a group to step into the battle as you . . .

- Thank God for the spiritual reality that he hears your prayers, he responds in power, and his Spirit lives in you and moves in real and recognizable ways when God's people pray.
- Think back on victories God has won on your behalf, times he has moved in power, and moments you have seen the Holy Spirit show up and do amazing things. Lift up prayers of praise for these specific moments in your life.
- Ask the Holy Spirit to fill, lead, and empower every member of your small group.
- Pray that your church will take prayer more seriously and that your leaders will commit to pray more and lead the congregation into deeper places of prayer.
- Think about a situation where you have prayed for a long time and still not seen results. Ask the Spirit of God to help you stay diligent in prayer and confident in faith that God will answer this prayer.

Prayer means persevering.
Sometimes you have to tie a knot
and hold on to the rope of prayer!

IN THE COMING DAYS

PERSONAL REFLECTION

Take time in personal reflection to think about the following
questions . . .

- What is getting in the way of me praying consistently and
  with bold confidence?
- What will help me make prayer a growing part of my life,
  friendships, and family?
- What are some ways I need to resist the devil and draw
  near to God?

Journal, Reflections, and Notes

Prayer connects us to the God who offers us the power we need to overcome every scheme, strategy, and attack of Satan, our enemy.

PERSONAL ACTIONS

Learning About the Holy Spirit

Take time in the coming weeks to read the entire book of Acts. Look for two specific themes throughout Acts and use the simple code below to indicate when you learn about one of these themes.

In the margin of your Bible, write (HS) every time you read about the presence, work, or movement of the Holy Spirit. Also, write (P) every time you see something powerful happen among Christians because of the presence and work of the Spirit of God.

Keep a journal in the space provided here to take note of what the Holy Spirit does, how he moves, and what happens when the Spirit is at work in the life of a Christian.

My Notes:

Passage where I see the Spirit present or at work:

What the Spirit does or how he moves:

What I learn for my life of faith:

Passage where I see the Spirit present or at work:

What the Spirit does or how he moves:

What I learn for my life of faith:

Passage where I see the Spirit present or at work:

What the Spirit does or how he moves:

What I learn for my life of faith:

Passage where I see the Spirit present or at work:

What the Spirit does or how he moves:

What I learn for my life of faith:

———————————

Passage where I see the Spirit present or at work:

What the Spirit does or how he moves:

What I learn for my life of faith:

Passage where I see the Spirit present or at work:

What the Spirit does or how he moves:

What I learn for my life of faith:

Passage where I see the Spirit present or at work:

What the Spirit does or how he moves:

What I learn for my life of faith:

Passage where I see the Spirit present or at work:

What the Spirit does or how he moves:

What I learn for my life of faith:

Passage where I see the Spirit present or at work:

What the Spirit does or how he moves:

What I learn for my life of faith:

Passage where I see the Spirit present or at work:

What the Spirit does or how he moves:

What I learn for my life of faith:

Praying for Power

➤ Jim reminded us that Christians need fresh filling with the power of the Holy Spirit day by day and moment by moment. Take time to write a prayer asking God to fill you with his power and fresh awareness of the Spirit's presence, power, and plan for your life.

My Prayer:

_____

_____

_____

_____

_____

_____

Lift up this prayer a few times each day for the coming week. Pray it with passion. Declare it with faith. Ask with expectation that you will be filled, again and again, with the renewing and glorious power of the Holy Spirit who dwells in you.

Victory comes through prayer.

Memorize and Personalize

Take time to commit Acts 1:8 to memory. Here it is:

> But you will receive power when the Holy Spirit comes on you;
> and you will be my witnesses in Jerusalem,
> and in all Judea and Samaria, and to the ends of the earth.

The disciples understood what Jesus was saying. Their source of power to impact and transform the whole world would come through the Holy Spirit of God, not from themselves. As they were filled with the Spirit, they would have courage, wisdom, and strength to bring the life-changing message of Jesus to four specific areas:

Jerusalem (Right where they were, their immediate neighborhood)

Judea (Their surrounding community and region)

Samaria (The tough places, often avoided places, the other side of the tracks)

The ends of the earth (Everywhere on the planet)

As you memorize and meditate on this powerful verse of the Bible, prayerfully declare your commitment to walk in the power of the Holy Spirit. Think about your Jerusalem, right where you live and work. Pray for your Judea, the community all around you and the region where you live. Offer to go to the places that many people avoid. Commit to share God's love and gospel with the marginalized and forgotten people around you . . . your Samaria. Then, dare to tell God that you will pray for the ends of the earth, give toward ministries that reach the ends of the earth, and even go to the ends of the earth if that is where God leads you.

Make this Scripture verse a life-commitment and declaration in a personal way.

I will receive power every time the Holy Spirit comes on me and I will be his witness and servant right where I live, in my greater community, in the tough and forgotten places, and anywhere the Spirt of God calls me to go. I will do this for the sake of Jesus and the world he loves and died to save, amen!

Build a Prayer Team

If you do not have two to four people who love Jesus, love you, and are committed to pray for you whenever you need support, commit to form a prayer team this week.

1. Pray about who you should invite to be on this small prayer team. Really seek the Lord and ask the Holy Spirit to put faces and names on your heart as you pray.

2. Make a list of these people and ask for the Spirit of God to prepare their hearts for your phone call or face-to-face meeting with them.

- _____

- _____

- _____

- _____

3. Connect with each of these people through a face-to-face meeting or voice-to-voice communication. Tell them that you are forming a prayer support team to surround you (and your family if you have one). Ask them if they would take a day or two and pray about committing to be a prayer support person in your life.

4. If someone says they are not feeling led to be on your prayer team, graciously thank them for praying about it and bless them for considering this opportunity.

5. For each person who says yes, thank them and assure them that when a situation arises that you need their partnership in prayer, you will contact them and share the need you are facing. If you have one or two specific areas of prayer support at the time to communicate with them, share the needs verbally and then follow up with a text, email, or note to remind them of the specific prayer needs.

6. As God answers prayer and shows up in power, be sure to contact your prayer team members and thank them for their prayers and share stories of how the Holy Spirit has moved in clear and wonderful ways.

One person praying is stronger than every demon in hell.

ADDITIONAL RESOURCES FOR GROUP LEADERS

Thank you for your willingness to lead a group through *Spiritual Warfare Is Real*. What you have chosen to do is important, and much good fruit can come from studies like this. The rewards of being a leader are different from those of participating, and we hope that as you lead you will find your own walk with Jesus deepened by this experience.

Spiritual Warfare Is Real is a five-session study built around video content and small-group interaction. As the group leader, imagine yourself as the host of a dinner party. Your job is to take care of your guests by managing all the behind-the-scenes details so that as your guests arrive, they can focus on each other and on interaction around the topic.

As the group leader, your role is *not* to answer all the questions or reteach the content—the video and study guide will do most of that work. Your job is to guide the experience and cultivate your small group into a kind of teaching community. This will make it a place for members to process, question, and reflect—not receive more instruction.

There are several elements in this leader's guide that will help you as you structure your study and reflection time, so follow along and take advantage of each one.

BEFORE YOU BEGIN

Before your first meeting, make sure the group members have a copy of this study guide so they can follow along and have their answers written out ahead of time. Alternately, you can hand out the study guides at your first meeting and give the group members some time to look over the material and ask any preliminary questions. During your first meeting, be sure to send a sheet around the room and have the members write down their name, phone number, and email address so you can keep in touch with them during the week.

Generally, the ideal size for a group is between eight to ten people, which ensures everyone will have enough time to participate in discussions. If you have more people, you might want to break up the main group into smaller subgroups. Encourage those who show up at the first meeting to commit to attending the duration of the study, as this will help the group members get to know each other, create stability for the group, and help you know how to prepare each week.

Each of the sessions begins with an opening reflection. The questions that follow in the "Talk About It" section serve as an icebreaker to get the group members thinking about the topic. Some people may want to tell a long story in response to one of these questions, but the goal is to keep the answers brief. Ideally, you want everyone in the group to get a chance to answer, so try to keep the responses to a minute or less. If you have talkative group members, say up front that everyone needs to limit the answer to one minute.

Give the group members a chance to answer, but tell them to feel free to pass if they wish. With the rest of the study, it's generally not a good idea to have everyone answer every question—a free-flowing discussion is more desirable. But with the opening icebreaker questions, you can go around the circle. Encourage shy people to share, but don't force them.

Before your first meeting, let the group members know that each session contains several between-sessions activities that they can complete during the week. While these are optional exercises, they will help the members cement the concepts presented during the group study time and encourage them to spend time each day in God's Word. Also invite members to bring any questions and insights they uncovered while reading to your next meeting, especially if they had a breakthrough moment or didn't understand something.

WEEKLY PREPARATION

As the leader, there are a few things you should do to prepare for each meeting:

- *Decide how video will be used.* Whether you are using the streaming video access on the inside front cover of this guide as a group or the DVD, decide if you want people to watch the video before or during the actual group time.
- *Read through the session.* This will help you to become familiar with the content and know how to structure the discussion times.

- *Decide which questions you definitely want to discuss.* Based on the amount and length of group discussion, you may not be able to get through all of the Bible study and group discussion questions, so choose four to five questions that you definitely want to cover.
- *Be familiar with the questions you want to discuss.* When the group meets, you'll be watching the clock, so you want to make sure you are familiar with the questions you have selected. In this way, you'll ensure you have the material more deeply in your mind than your group members.
- *Pray for your group.* Pray for your group members throughout the week and ask God to lead them as they study his Word.
- *Bring extra supplies to your meeting.* The members should bring their own pens for writing notes, but it's a good idea to have extras available for those who forget. You may also want to bring paper and additional Bibles.

Note that in many cases there will be no one "right" answer to the question the group will be discussing. Answers will vary, especially when the group members are being asked to share their personal experiences.

STRUCTURING THE DISCUSSION TIME

You will need to determine with your group how long you want to meet each week so you can plan your time accordingly. Generally, most groups like to meet for either sixty minutes or ninety minutes, so you could use one of the following schedules:

Section	60 Minutes	90 Minutes
WELCOME (members arrive and get settled)	5 minutes	10 minutes
ICEBREAKER (discuss one or both of opening questions for the session)	10 minutes	15 minutes
VIDEO (watch the teaching segment and take notes, unless group has already watched the video)	15 minutes	15 minutes
DISCUSSION (discuss the Bible study questions you selected ahead of time)	25 minutes	40 minutes
PRAYER/CLOSING (pray together as a group and dismiss)	5 minutes	10 minutes

As the group leader, it is up to you to keep track of the time and keep things moving along according to your schedule. You might want to set a timer for each segment so both you and the group members know when your time is up. (Note there are some good phone apps for timers that play a gentle chime or other pleasant sound instead of a disruptive noise.)

Don't be concerned if the group members are quiet or slow to share. People are often quiet when they are pulling together their ideas, and this might be a new experience for them. Just ask a question and let it hang in the air until someone shares. You can then say, "Thank you. What about others? What came to you when you watched that portion of the video?"

GROUP DYNAMICS

Leading a group through *Spiritual Warfare Is Real* will prove to be highly rewarding both to you and your group members. However, this doesn't mean you will not encounter any challenges along the way! Discussions can get off track. Group members may not be sensitive to the needs and ideas of others. Some might worry they will be expected to talk about matters that make them feel awkward. Others may express comments that result in disagreements. To help ease this strain on you and the group, consider the following ground rules:

- When someone raises a question or comment that is off the main topic, suggest you deal with it another time, or, if you feel led to go in that direction, let the group know you will be spending some time discussing it.
- If someone asks a question you don't know how to answer, admit it and move on. At your discretion, feel free to invite group members to comment on questions that call for personal experience.
- If you find one or two people are dominating the discussion time, direct a few questions to others in the group. Outside the main group time, ask the more dominating members to help you draw out the quieter ones. Work to make them a part of the solution instead of the problem.
- When a disagreement occurs, encourage the group members to process the matter in love. Encourage those on opposite sides to restate what they heard the other side say about the matter, and then invite each side to evaluate if that perception is accurate. Lead the group in examining other Scriptures related to the topic and look for common ground.

When any of these issues arise, encourage your group members to follow these words from the Bible: "Love one another"

(John 13:34), "If it is possible, as far as it depends on you, live at peace with everyone" (Romans 12:18), and "Be quick to listen, slow to speak and slow to become angry" (James 1:19). This will make your group time more rewarding and beneficial for everyone who attends.

Thank you again for your willingness to lead your group. May God reward your efforts and dedication and make your time together in *Spiritual Warfare Is Real* fruitful for his kingdom.

God's throne of grace. It is not a physical location you can visit, but the promises you read about it in the Bible are so immense that they are almost beyond belief. And as Hebrews 4:16 states, you can always "approach God's throne of grace with confidence," knowing that you will "receive mercy and find grace" to help you in your time of need.

Pastor Jim Cymbala explores how God promises in his Word to always hear you, answer you, and extend his mercy when you come to him. As you pray with faith, you will find that approaching God's throne of grace will change your life and circumstances like nothing else—and that when you and other believers call on his name, powerful things happen in the world!

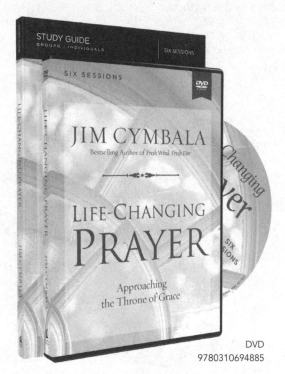

Study Guide
9780310694847

DVD
9780310694885

Available now at your favorite bookstore,
or streaming video on StudyGateway.com

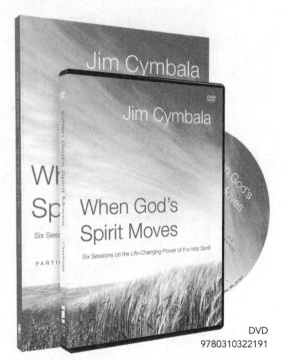

For anyone seeking to live at the center of God's purposes, this well-loved book points the way to new spiritual vitality in the church and in your own life.

A classic must-read for readers looking for hope and transformation in the church today, *Fresh Wind, Fresh Fire* shows what the Holy Spirit can do when believers get serious about prayer and the gospel. As this compelling book reveals, God moves in life-changing ways—calling us back from spiritual dead ends, apathy, and lukewarm religion—when we set aside our own agendas, take him at his word, and listen for his voice.

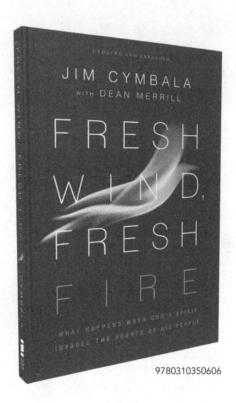

9780310350606

Available now at your favorite bookstore.

ZONDERVAN®

We Need God's Power

Drawing examples from the Bible and from the sidewalks of New York City, *Fresh Power* shows what happens when the Spirit of God moves in our midst. He longs to reveal the mind of God to us and to release heaven's limitless resources to meet the desperate needs around us. *Fresh Power* will expand your vision for what God can and will do, and inspire you to pray like never before for God's power in your church—and in you.

9780310251545

Available now at your favorite bookstore.

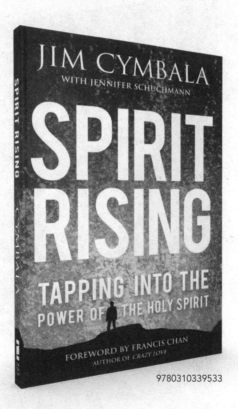

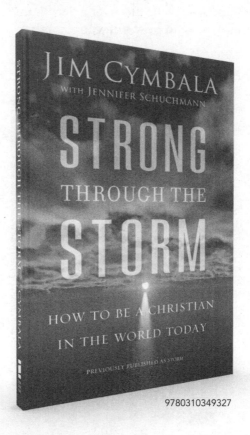